Milton Horn, *Sculptor*

Milton Horn, 1982

Milton Horn

Sculptor

16 March – 30 July, 1989

Spertus Museum of Judaica
Chicago, Illinois

Milton Horn, Sculptor was prepared on the occasion of the artist's retrospective exhibition on view at Spertus Museum of Judaica from March 16–July 30, 1989. This exhibit has been organized by Spertus Museum of Judaica.

This exhibiton and catalogue were made possible through major grants from the Illinois Arts Council, the Chicago Office of Fine Arts, and the generosity of an individual donor, Budwin Conn.

Folio
NB
237
H67
A4
1989

Front cover: ADAM (detail from HYMN TO WATER), 1961–65
Bronze relief, H: 198 cm (78")
Collection of the artist.

Back cover: 'Woman's Head, "Chicago"' (detail from CHICAGO RISING FROM THE LAKE), 1954
Bronze high relief
Façade of City of Chicago Parking Facility #1, Chicago.

The Spertus College Press, Chicago, Illinois 60605

Spertus College is a beneficiary of the Jewish Federation of Metropolitan Chicago. This exhibit is partially supported by a grant from the Illinois Arts Council, a state agency.

All photos appearing in this catalogue were taken by Estelle Horn with the following exceptions: page 2 by Vic Haines; pages 62 and 63 by P. J. Gates Ltd, London.

Catalogue design by James Shurmer, in association with Graham Johnson, Mike Brehm and Mark Akgulian.

Phototypeset in Monotype Lasercomp Baskerville by Southern Positives and Negatives (SPAN), Lingfield, Surrey. Printed and bound in the UK by Balding and Mansell.

Contents

Milton and Estelle Horn in his studio during the modeling of CHICAGO RISING FROM THE LAKE, Chicago, 1954.

Artist's Acknowledgement

My statement is my work, the unseen element being my appreciation and gratitude to the multitude of people who have supported me with their love and understanding: to Estelle, my wife and collaborator who for 49 years through her superlative photography bore witness until her death in 1975 to the complete metamorphosis of my work. The majority of photographs in this exhibition and catalogue are hers; to Paula and Peter Ellis who after Estelle's death challenged and provoked me back to the poem with renewed force and conviction; to Paula for her commitment to this exhibition and for her efforts in producing a video documentary of my life and work; and finally to my many other friends who have contributed tirelessly over the years to my personal creative well-being: Urban Couch, Robert Hertzberg, Catherine Malcori, Dr. Patricia McCreary, Ms. Sidney Dent, Judge and Mrs. Alfred Teton, Diana Iseberg, Dr. Bernard Rappaport, C. E. Silling, K. Boles-Wertz, Dr. Milton Levine, Dr. Susan Engel-Ariel, Budwin Conn, my late sister, Esther Zimmerer and my brothers and sisters.

(Detail from TORAH ARK DOORS), 1959–60
White oak, direct carving
Temple B'nai Israel, Charleston, West Virginia
(cat. 43).

Foreword

by Dr. Morris A. Fred

Director, Spertus Museum of Judaica

The mythmakers' responsibility to the spiritual needs of the community is the heartbeat of the creative act. Man will go to science for new concepts of space and for the means to ease and prolong his physical life, but in order to save himself from spiritual genocide and remain *man*, whom God has made only 'a little lower than the angels,' he will come to the mythopoet for the eternal dialogue.

Milton Horn, 1957

Since the dawn of the twentieth century, artists have struggled to capture through the creative process a spiritual alternative to the increasing technology and materialism of modern society. Originally, much of this art was outside the bounds of religious traditions often expressing the artist's alienation from an industrialized world. In recent years, artists – young and old – have increasingly returned to their religious roots as a nurturing matrix for their artistic creativity. As a teacher and artist, Milton Horn is one of the pioneers of this movement. His sculpture, reliefs and drawings spring from his innermost passion to express through biblical, secular and mythological images both his humanism and his emotional and intellectual link to Judaism.

Thus, this exhibition becomes more than just a survey of an artist's career focusing on formal concerns; it is, rather, a record of the artist's spiritual journey examining the emotive potential of each creation. In addition, it represents our efforts here at Spertus Museum of Judaica to create an open forum where contemporary artists can express and communicate their individual responses to what it means and has meant to be a Jew, confronting our audience with a wide range of diverse issues relevant to the understanding of fundamental values and precepts inherent in the Jewish tradition. Finally, in this exhibition, we acknowledge the stimulus of the City of Chicago, renown for its public art and architecture, and its inspiration to an artist whose creations have become a part of this city's ambience.

This celebration of a major figure in American sculpture has been all the more significant to those of us at Spertus Museum who have come to know Milton Horn. It has been a privilege to work with an artist whose humanitarian philosophy is revealed not only in his work, but also in his life. Responses from friends and colleagues on both sides of the Atlantic confirm his contribution to contemporary sculpture and his unique gift for inspiring devotion.

In conclusion, I would like to express my appreciation to those many individuals who have contributed to this exhibition: to those who have graciously loaned objects; to Paula Garrett Ellis for her tireless energy in aiding co-curators Mark Akgulian and Olga Weiss in organizing the exhibition; to Harold Haydon for his excellent essay: to Dr. Susan Engel-Arieli and William Johnstone who together with Paula Garrett Ellis helped coordinate efforts to gain support for this project; and finally to Budwin Conn and the following contributors whose generosity made this catalogue possible: Lee R. Hamilton, Dr. Judith Lichtenstein, Drs. Laura and Paul Mesaros, Thomas F. Pado, Ronald Sherman, Mary and Theodore Silverstein, and the West Virginia University Foundation.

Milton Horn carving CONSECRATION OF ISAIAH, Chicago, 1951.

Milton Horn, Sculptor

by Harold Haydon

Harold Haydon, a painter and muralist, is Professor Emeritus of Art, University of Chicago, and served as Art Critic for the Chicago Sun–Times, 1963–85.

Mankind's dreams and aspirations, the loves and hopes of triumphant living, traditionally find expression in the arts, and in none so tangibly and intimately as in the art of sculpture.

Stone, metal, clay, wood and plaster, shaped by the mind and hands of the sculptor can embody the full range of human experience, from the most sensitive portrait to those grand monuments that memorialize our finest moments and greatest achievements.

Not every sculptor is equipped by training, skill, temperament, and depth of feeling to create works of the highest quality. In fact, it can be argued that there is likely to be only one Michelangelo in a century, and in all the arts perhaps no more than a half-dozen of the first rank at one time.

Therefore, it may come as a surprise to find Milton Horn considered as one of the elect, a sculptor whose high standards, personal integrity, and spiritual dedication to the artist's role as myth-maker set him apart. According to ancient Hebrew legend, thirty-six saints grace every generation. If so, Milton Horn must be a leader in his time.

The evidence is two-fold. First, he is an original who has ignored contemporary mainstream art and has been known to strike out against it. At the same time he has been thoroughly professional and has not gone unnoticed, exhibiting widely and in such major museums as the Metropolitan Museum of Art and the Whitney Museum of American Art in New York, and the Art Institute of Chicago. He has been honored by the National Academy of Design, the National Sculpture Society, the Sculptors Guild, and the American Institute of Architects. His work is in the permanent collections of the National Museum of American Art, Washington, D.C., the National Academy of Design, New York City, and the Brookgreen Gardens, Charleston, South Carolina. Many commissioned works are in religious, civic, educational, corporate and private hands.

Secondly, Horn's sculptural affinities span the ages and, I suspect, foreshadow the future. He has always found roots and sustenance in great art of the past. In all, he found basic principles that link the past, present, and no doubt the future of sculpture as an ongoing cultural necessity. Yet he is not an eclectic artist. He did not adopt a style, or leap onto anyone's bandwagon. From all his studies he extracted the essence that became purely his own and gives his work consistency in point of view and practice.

In his twenties, he 'became aware that the greatest sculptures of the ancients were originally an integral part of architecture or related to it, that the proportions and forms of these sculptures were an organic outgrowth from the problems and the spiritual needs of the people, and that style is not preconceived but develops organically, like a fruit.'[1]

Propitiously, Horn's first major commission, in 1927, was for a ceiling sculpture in low relief for the Lentheric Salon in New York City's Savoy-Plaza Hotel, demolished in 1940. The ceiling of the long, narrow room was bordered by Art Deco geometric repeat patterns of the sort that Horn long since had rejected. Seeking a more humane and original motif, he chose the human figure, male and

---

[1] Milton Horn, Biographical Data, 1965.

female nudes varying in size to fit the space. 'I had learned the principles from the Romanesque sculptors,' Horn said.[2]

He responded to the architectural setting by combining the flowing curves outlining the figures with angular elements echoing the Art Deco forms. In this first important commission he established the reciprocal relations between sculpture and architecture that he adhered to throughout his subsequent career and which have served him well.

That achievement was not lost on the critics. Talbot Hamlin, for one, reproduced the Lentheric Salon ceiling in *Pencil Points*, December, 1938, with an article titled 'Form and Content: Contemporary Architectural Sculpture in America,' and again in 'Forms and Functions in 20th Century Architecture,' Columbia University Press, 1952. The ceiling with its then-daring figuration established the young sculptor's reputation.

Born near Kiev, Russia, September 1, 1906, Milton Horn arrived in Taunton, Massachusetts with his family in 1913, and became an American citizen in 1917. In 1922, the Horns moved to New York City. Milton had classes in drawing and painting from the age of 12, turning to sculpture in the 1920's.

In 1925, he won a Tiffany Foundation Fellowship that gave him a summer at the Foundation in Oyster Bay, Long Island, making sculptural studies from nature, drawing, and steeping himself in Oriental art.

In 1928, Horn married the young dancer Estelle Oxenhorn, who became a talented photographer and was an invaluable aid to the sculptor until her death in 1975. A fine artist in her own right, Estelle devoted her life to furthering Milton's career, caring for correspondence, keeping files, and recording with her camera the stages of his sculptures as they progressed from inception to completion.

[2] Milton Horn, 'Introduction to the Milton and Estelle Horn Collection.'

Depression years brought new opportunities, including work at the Brooklyn Museum, cataloguing and designing mounts for antiquities in the Wilbur Collection with its Egyptian sculpture, and dating and restoring the museum's Coptic textiles. A WPA commission in 1935 led to Horn's first woodcarvings, six large mahogany reliefs for a New York City high school. The next two years brought commissions from the United States Department of the Treasury for post office murals in relief sculpture.

Horn began a productive decade in 1939 by accepting appointment as sculptor-in-residence at Olivet College, Olivet, Michigan, under a Carnegie Corporation grant. At the request of the college, the grant was renewed for another year, and in 1941 the college made him Professor of Art and Sculptor-in-Residence, a position he held until he resigned in 1949 to concentrate on sculpture.

Another post office commission for relief sculpture, featuring Paul Bunyan, was followed in 1943 by a commission for a large cherrywood relief that brought Horn into working relations with Frank Lloyd Wright, architect of the C. D. Wall residence in Plymouth, Michigan, where the sculpture flanks a fireplace. The collaboration of sculptor and architect in designing and lighting the relief perfectly exemplified the oneness that Horn holds to be central in the mythopoetic function of sculpture. Architecture was modified to enhance sculpture as sculpture responded to architecture. Together, architect and sculptor determined the rhythmic flow of forms and textures in space.

These Olivet years yielded many fine works. Outstanding is the kneeling figure of 'Job,' five feet high, modeled directly in plaster for casting in bronze. The emaciated, long-suffering, righteous man, head thrown back and gazing upward, may be hearing the voice of God speaking from the whirlwind. Rough surfaced, catching light dramatically, 'Job' is one of Horn's best known works, having been shown first in 1948–49 at the Jewish Museum in New York City, in the Philadelphia Museum of Art in 1949, the Art Institute of Chicago in 1950, the Metropolitan Museum of Art in 1951, and elsewhere. Although the original plaster was destroyed in an Italian foundry, two casts were made in bronze. One is in the National Museum of American Art; the other, in a private collection, is lent for this exhibition.

Another important woodcarving, 'Metamorphosis No. 1,' inspired by a poem by Ovid and completed in 1949, was first exhibited at the Whitney Museum in 1949, and in Chicago's Art Institute in 1950. Carved directly in walnut, the relief stands nearly six feet high. The rich, flowing forms of figures and foliage course upward with the vigor and complexity of large and small shapes that are characteristic of Horn's work.

Even a single figure in the round, for example the bronze 'Bathsheba' of 1948, only 14 inches high, organizes the space it occupies with rhythmically intertwining volumes of limbs and torso, and carefully studied voids, that infuse the figure with the spirit of life.

By the time he left Olivet for Chicago in 1949, Milton Horn was in full stride, principled and certain of his path. 'Great works of sculpture, no matter what their iconography, transcend time, place, and cult and become the valued spiritual heritage of mankind,' he said.[3] Horn brought this conviction to whatever he touched, whether a Biblical subject for a synagogue, a secular symbol for a city, an image for a school or university, an allegory or mythological theme, even a portrait.

Just as he had discovered the intimate interplay of formal and emotive elements in sculpture and architecture early in his career, he was very young when, talking

---

[3] Milton Horn, 'Biography of One of America's Foremost Sculptors' Medical Heritage Society, 1971.

FAIRY TALES, 1949
Bass wood relief
Blythe Park School,
Riverside, Illinois
(cat. 25).

with his father who was a Talmudic scholar, he first became aware of the poetry and legends of the Jewish people and the mythmaking functions of art. In his Chicago period he brought these insights to bear on the conception and execution of the many important commissions entrusted to his hands.

In 1950–51, Horn embarked on one of the great adventures of his lifetime, the creation of a limestone relief, 12 by 10 feet, for the exterior of West Surburban Temple Har Zion, River Forest, Illinois, northwest of Chicago. Above the inscription, 'Not by Might nor by Power, but by My Spirit Saith the Lord of Hosts' is a gigantic seated figure holding the Tablets of the Law. This figure, one of the guardian Cherubim, who took many forms, has the body of a man and a head with four eyes engulfed by flames, signifying the Divine Presence (Shekhinah). The Cherub presses down on Behemoth, subduing the symbol of brutishness and ignorance. For the first time, so far as is known, a human form appeared on the exterior of a synagogue. The sculpture was noticed around the world.

In 1932–35 well-preserved ruins of a synagogue built in 245 C.E. were discovered at Dura-Europos, a former city on the Euphrates. Paintings portraying scenes and people from the Bible showed that a Jewish pictorial art had existed. Also, the mosaic floor of a 6th Century synagogue with ritual symbols and a depiction of the sacrifice of Isaac had been unearthed in the Valley of Jezreel in 1922, but these were pictorial representations inside the synagogue.

Sculpture is another, quite different matter. 'Sculpture inhabits actual space in all its dimensions,' Horn says. 'Since it lives in space, sculpture interacts with space, measures and is measured by it.'[4] Such tangibility can have theological consequences. It took great courage for a 20th century sculptor to defy the traditional ban on graven images.

The impressive figure was carved directly in stone by the sculptor, who had assistance in roughing out the image but trusted no one but himself to achieve the subtleties in modeling forms and textures required by his conception. By carving

[4] Milton Horn, Catalogue 'Sculpture by Horn.' Olivet College, 1948.

Mural, Carleton D. Wall
residence, 1943–44
Cherrywood incised relief
Residence was designed
by architect
Frank Lloyd Wright,
Plymouth, Michigan
(cat. 16).

directly in stone Horn broke with the Beaux Arts tradition in which the sculptor modeled in clay but left the stone cutting to others.

Again, in 1959, Horn introduced the human image where, to the best of his knowledge, it had not appeared before, serving as the vehicle for the voice of God when He spoke to Moses from the Burning Bush. The occasion was a bronze relief, 8 feet, 6 inches high by 5 feet, 6 inches, commissioned for the exterior of B'nai Israel Temple, Charleston, West Virginia, with the title 'And the Angel of the Lord Appeared to Him in a Flame of Fire Out of the Midst of a Bush.'

Also in 1951, Horn completed one of his most important woodcarvings, 'The Consecration of Isaiah,' nearly 8 by 4 feet, carved directly in walnut. The prophet is kneeling in the foreground, arms raised and looking up. Above Isaiah is a Seraph, the Angel of the Lord who purged Isaiah of sin by touching a live coal from the altar to his lips. The head of the Seraph combines man, eagle, bull and lion. Above all, looking down from on high, is the face of God, partially veiled by smoke from the altar.

In work after work, Horn has used the human figure, avowedly as a necessary adjunct to full expression, saying 'I have never lost sight of that mythopoetic character of sculpture and its figural representation which has given aesthetic reality and emotional and intellectual power to my works.'[5]

What is true for his Biblical and ritual subjects is true also for his secular sculpture. The spiritual content must be in them too. Essentially, Horn's sculpture is public art, whether made for a Jewish house of worship, the City of Chicago, a medical center, the Continental Can Company, a school, or a residence. The mythopoetic aspect of his sculpture also is apparent and important in those works such as 'Pain,' 'Birth of a Poet,' the 'Metamorphoses,' and the 'Dancers,' created for his own collection and for exhibition, any one of which, like 'Job,' may in time become public art in a museum collection.

[5] Milton Horn, 'Introduction to the Milton and Estelle Horn Collection.'

Horn's first City of Chicago commission, the three-ton bronze 'Chicago Rising from the Lake,' 12 by 14 feet in high relief, was modeled and cast in 1954–55. For 28 years it graced the north façade of Parking Facility No. 1 at Wacker Drive and North Dearborn, until the building was demolished in 1983 to make way for North Loop development, causing the scheduled relocation of the sculpture on the Civic Opera Building, 20 N. Wacker Drive.

Chicago is symbolized by a gently smiling female figure holding a sheaf of grain and flanked by a bull and an eagle representing the city's pre-eminence as a commodities market, its once-active stockyards, and its role as a transportation center. Foliage is a reminder of Chicago's motto, 'Urbs in Horta,' the city in a garden.

A second city commission in 1963, completed in 1965, called for a monumental bronze relief for the lobby of the Administration Building of the Central Water Filtration Plant on the lakefront north of Navy Pier. 'Hymn to Water,' 10 feet high and 24 feet long, is Horn's largest single work. It is rich in imagery drawn from lore and legend associated with water.

In a composition of dominant horizontals, few verticals and sweeping diagonals, the giant figure of the Diety is central, reaching down from a heaven of clouds, mist, and fire to model Man from dust mixed with water as Man sits with his feet in waters teeming with life.

The sun, on the right, draws water from the sea to form clouds that pour rain on a luxuriant tree under which a man and a woman gather the fruits of the sea and land. On the left, the moon exerts its tidal powers, even drawing Leviathan up with the water. Vegetation and creatures of sea, land, and air fill out the complex design. The huge relief was cast in twenty sections and welded together.

Every artist of stature has unrealized projects, sometimes beyond the resources and imagination of his time. Such dreams may be developed as plans on paper and models in clay, plaster, wood and other materials. In 1961, at a time of general urban renewal, Horn proposed the sculpture 'Mother City: Chicago Emerging from the Fire,' a lyrical figure of a woman with an owl, executed in plaster 36 inches high for casting in bronze. It was intended for a 'conversation plaza' of Horn's design. Although that project did not materialize, the sculpture has independent existence.

Another Horn proposal is for a colossal figure of a patriarch, rising 90 feet tall from the waves of Lake Michigan in Chicago's watery dooryard, titled '. . . Who Walketh Upon the Wings of the Wind.' As with other proposals executed on a small scale, the model may appear too condensed, too complex, and too energetic; it must be imagined at full scale to assess its effect. Should this conception be realized, Chicago will have acquired a visual presence of Biblical stature, a symbol with boundless energy to match the famed dynamic vigor of the metropolis. More than this, as with so much of Horn's imagery, the enormous figure conveys a spiritual grace and harmony of parts that could serve as a formative force, defining the city's meaning for its people. That is reason enough for sculpture.

With his devotion to the human form as the primary vehicle for the expression of emotion and transfer of thought, Horn stands squarely in the centuries-old tradition of Western art, and of most of the world's art. The doors to the subtleties and complexities of the human spirit stand open to the sculptor who can master the language of gesture and facial expression.

In this exhibition Horn's command over the range of human expression is amply demonstrated in his portraits and in his figure drawings. These virtuoso drawings are of two sorts. The line drawings with brush or pen and ink adopt an Oriental method but not an Oriental style, having been drawn directly, with no preliminary sketch or guidelines. Their measure of success depends on the artist's knowledge of the figure, his eye, and manual skill. Verisimilitude is less important than the spacing, flow, and rhythmic qualities of line, while the artist's ability to capture the living essence of the figure is all-important. The other sort of drawings consists of particular views of sculpture, often worked out in light and shade, as the means of studying sculptural problems. In both kinds of drawing, Horn reveals the distinctive qualities of line and composition that are found also in his sculpture. Characteristically, he combines rhythmic, curvilinear movement of form with contrasting angularities of line and contour.

Throughout his long career Milton Horn has shown consistently his love and respect for life. The intimacy of mother and child, as in 'Bathsheba and Solomon;' the struggle of man with the Divine, as in 'Job,' the 'Ascension of Rabbi Judah,' and in 'I Will Not Let Thee Go,' portraying Jacob wrestling with the Angel; and the joys and sorrows of womanhood seen in other works; all are aspects of the human condition that have moved the sculptor to create.

Everything is summed up in one late great bronze titled 'God and Israel.' In this work two winged figures are found in passionate embrace in a circular composition that builds form upon form without loss of coherence. 'God and Israel' can be grasped at many levels of meaning, from a visual love poem celebrating the union of man and woman to the spiritual wedding of humanity and Divinity. It may well be the sculptor's finest work.

This first restrospective survey of Milton Horn's lifetime in sculpture assembles full-size woodcarvings and bronzes, models and photographs of major works *in situ* never before seen together. The effect is overwhelming, proof that Horn in his chosen field stands alone in his time.

Chicago, November 1988

Interview with Milton Horn
by Paula Garrett Ellis

I first met Milton Horn late in his career. He was 75 years old when he began working on a portrait of me, and at the same time, in a funny kind of turnabout, I was trying to do a portrait of him on video tape. My purpose wasn't to record the facts of his life, but to visually explore the man and the sources of his art.

Following are a few unedited excerpts from the documentary entitled, 'The Message of Form, Milton Horn, The Sculptor, The Man.'

Paula   You have often stated that all great works of art and architecture have something in common; can you describe this commonality and how it has influenced your career?

Milton   'I have a private collection . . . of Gothic, Chinese, African sculpture of various periods . . .

'Out of them I've learned and found that all great sculptors in the world . . . observed similar things, follow similar principles.

'They all knew that anatomy had nothing to do with sculpture, that how light falls on bronze or on stone or wood is different, and they realized that by creating the large planes on which light falls . . . they defined an inner structure. The structure of a piece of sculpture is quite different from the structure of a human being, although it may evoke a thing or a human form.'

'Whenever a sculptor used numerous forms . . . they were not a conglomeration of objects, they became one . . . All these forms become an organic part of the whole of a completely new organism . . . sculpture must always become a complete new organism . . .'

'The way you can recognize a fruit, whether it's ripe or raw, you can recognize a work of art which is arrived at, which has gone through the process of metamorphosis and grown.'

Paula   Milton, I know that it is important for you to be identified as a universal artist, but please tell me how Judaism specifically affected your work?

Milton   'Judaism affected my work because in it I saw the same principles that I found when I looked at a great work of art: organization, the inter-relationship, the creation of one form that could exist and transcend time. And that was a thing that I felt from my earliest youth.'

'When I lived with my grandfather, I was taken every Saturday afternoon to the synagogue where, before the evening services, the old men would gather around and talk, tell tales. The tales were based on the scripture passage of the week, but it was not a theological discussion. It became for them a point of departure for the creation of a new legend.

'It was a very interesting thing which I could not understand at that time, but now at my mature age as I look back, it was a sense of building, in their isolation, for them a sense of aristocracy, a sense of tradition, a great sense of nobility.'

'In my early childhood I heard the great poems of my people.'

'And the years went on, I drew more and more sustenance from the poem . . . I felt that I had to communicate that poem with someone . . . somehow, more than an abstract idea, it had to have also, to me, a tactile sense . . .'

'I have chosen the poems, the ancient poems of my people, as starting points for some of these things.'

'. . . I have also realized one thing, that I must give that image not of one people, but of all people. And that poem is not the poem of my people alone, it is the poem of all mankind.'

Paula At what point do myths, poems and the visual arts interesect?

Milton 'The myth is the image man creates, either in verbal or in visual form, in which he tries to explain or to evoke in man an answer for the unanswerable . . .'

'And a work of art is, in the last rung, a denial of aloneness. It is a sharing. It is a shedding, a sheddding of love, an embrace of all those that come in contact with it.'

Video:
'The Message of Form, Milton Horn, The Sculptor, The Man'
1989 30 minutes
Produced by Paula Garrett Ellis

On the Nature of Sculpture

by Milton Horn

The function of sculpture is not to decorate but to integrate, not to entertain but to orientate man within the context of his universe.

Sculpture inhabits actual space in all its dimensions, and by its own inherent structural logic is able to impress upon our imagination a sense of reality. Whether it be an integral part of an architectural structure or free standing in architectural space or among nature's forms its sets up an inter-relationship between itself and its surroundings. Like life its myriad views assume new aspects under varying conditions; like life it is capable of drawing upon itself new interpretations and transcending them. Since it lives in actual space it interacts with it, measures it and is measured by it. The structure, the density or the translucency of the material, the specific life the work is to live, the rhythms of the time, which engulf the sculptor, join in the interaction and set up relationships that exist between the component parts of the work and the whole, between the whole and its surroundings.

Sculpture is not an ersatz for man, beast, bird or any of these put together arbitrarily. Though it draws from nature structural principles, its functions are as totally different as its materials are. Transcending their physical properties, within the realm of our imagination, sculptured forms assume an aspect of the inter-dependence of all in the making of the ONE.

Sculpture is composed of concrete material interacting with thought, thought which draws its nourishment from experience with form. When concrete material and thought interact with space the resultant forms, in one way or another, recall either nature's forms or formalized aspects of nature's forms. Though sculptured forms live totally different lives from the motifs which they resemble, there is no such thing as non-representational, three dimensional form, and yet sculpture by its very nature is an abstraction. Like architecture it is an organic abstraction in concrete form. When sculpture is wed to the architectural structure or wed to nature's forms and the topography of the site-sculpture wed to any or all of these performs the function of integrating man spiritually to his universe.

Olivet College, Olivet, Michigan. June, 1948

The Plates

ESTELLE, 1933, bronze, H: 45.7 cm (18″). Collection of the artist (cat. 6).

(*Opposite page*) SUMMER, 1938, terra cotta, 85.1 cm × 50.1 cm ($33\frac{1}{2}'$ × $19\frac{3}{4}''$). Collection of the artist (cat. 9).

PAUL BUNYAN STRAIGHTENING OUT THE ROUND RIVER, 1941
Maplewood relief, direct carving
152 cm × 148 cm (5′ × 4′ 9″)
United States Post Office, Iron River, Michigan
(cat. 13).

THE SPIRIT OF THE MAIL, 1938
Teakwood relief, direct carving
137 cm × 106 cm (4′ 6″ × 3′ 6″)
United States Post Office, Swarthmore, Pennsylvania
(cat. 11).

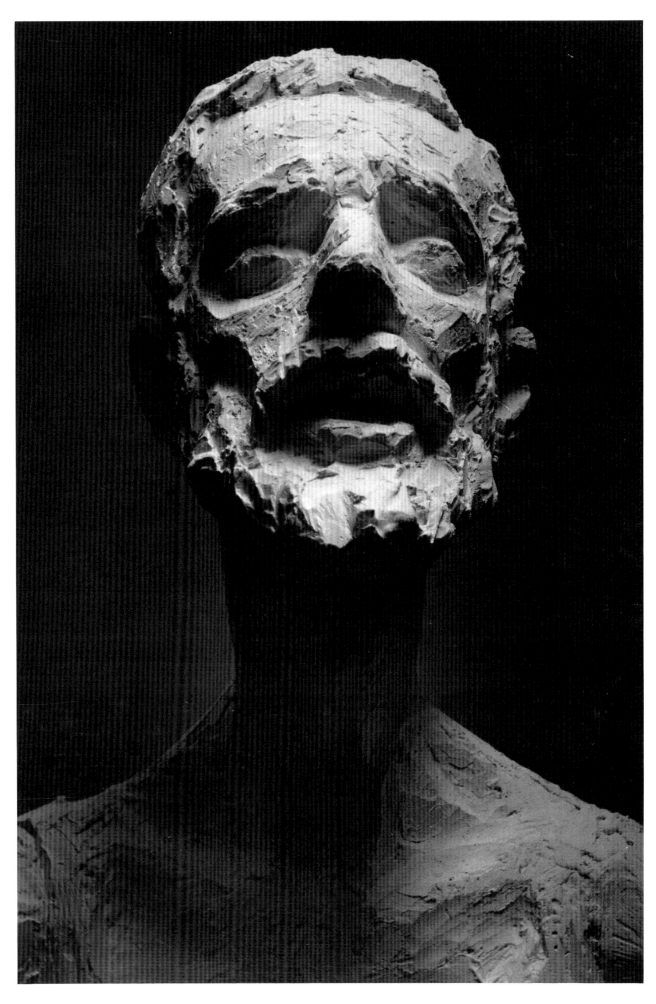

JOB (Book of Job 13:15), 1947, bronze. H: 152 cm (60″). Collection of Tod J. and Timothy M. Kaufman (cat. 18).

BATHSHEBA, 1948, bronze, H: 35.5 cm (14″). Collection of Dr. and Mrs. Robert Wertz (cat. 20).

MOTHER AND CHILD IN A GARDEN, 1948, (revised, 1967), plaster, H: 165 cm (5′ 5″)
Collection of the artist (cat. 22).

COMPOSITION, 1944
Alabaster high relief, direct carving
H: 26.6 cm (10½")
Collection of the artist
(cat.15).

METAMORPHOSIS II, 1949
Walnut wood relief,
direct carving
81.2 cm × 40.5 cm (32″ × 16″)
Collection of the artist
(cat. 24).

'NOT BY MIGHT, NOR BY POWER, BUT BY MY SPIRIT SAITH THE LORD OF HOSTS' (Zechariah 4:6), 1950
Limestone relief
366 cm × 305 cm (12' × 10')
West Suburban Temple Har Zion, River Forest, Illinois

'NOT BY MIGHT, NOR BY POWER, BUT BY MY SPIRIT SAITH THE LORD OF HOSTS' (Zechariah 4:6), 1950
Plaster
179 cm × 155 cm (70½″ × 61″)
Collection of the artist.

HALACHA, 1950
Bronze
H: 58 cm (23″)
Collection of the artist
(cat. 26).

LAMENTATIONS I, 1951
Nickel silver
H: 41 cm (16⅛″)
Collection of Barrie and Tod J. Kaufman
(cat. 31).

(*Above and left*) CONSECRATION OF ISAIAH, 1951
Walnut wood relief, direct carving, 245 cm × 120 cm ($96\frac{1}{4}''$ × $47\frac{1}{4}''$).
Collection of the artist (cat. 30).

(*Above and left*) TORAH ARK, 1954, mahogany wood relief, direct carving, 450 cm × 360 cm (15′ × 12′)
Collection Congregation Kol Ami (formerly South Shore Temple), Chicago (cat. 35).

HISTORY OF MEDICINE, 1954–56
Eight marble reliefs (on four pylons)
223 cm × 97 cm (88″ × 38″)
Medical Center, University of West Virginia, Morgantown, West Virginia
(cat. 37).

(*Left*) 'Hippocrates and Aristotle (460–370 BC)' (*Right*) 'X-ray Fluroscope' from HISTORY OF MEDICINE, 1954–56
223.5 cm × 96.5 cm (88″ × 38″)
Medical Center, University of West Virginia, Morgantown, West Virginia (cat. 37).

CHICAGO RISING FROM THE LAKE, 1954
Bronze high relief
366 cm × 426 cm (12′ × 14′)
City of Chicago Parking Facility #1, Chicago (building demolished in 1983)
(cat. 36c).

TORAH ARK DOORS, 1959–60
White oak, direct carving
198 cm × 162 cm (6′ 6″ × 5′ 4″)
Temple B'nai Israel, Charleston, West Virginia
(cat. 43).

(*Above and right*) ARK-REREDOS, 1957–58, Limba wood, direct carving, 334 cm × 152 cm (11′ × 6′)
Collection of the Rebecca Silling Chapel (All Faiths) Medical Center, University of West Virginia, Morgantown, West Virginia (cat. 38).

48

(Above and left)
MOSES BEFORE THE BURNING BUSH, bronze relief, 259 cm × 167 cm ($8\frac{1}{2}' \times 5\frac{1}{2}'$)
Temple B'nai Israel, Charleston, West Virginia (cat. 42).

DANCER II, 1960
Bronze
H: 47 cm (18½")
Collection of the artist
(cat. 45).

MOTHER CITY: CHICAGO EMERGING FROM THE FIRE, 1961
Plaster, H: 90.2 cm $(35\frac{1}{2}'')$. Collection of the artist (cat. 46).

THE ASCENSION OF RABBI JUDAH, 1963, bronze relief, 127 cm × 914 cm (50″ × 36″)
West Suburban Temple Har Zion, River Forest, Illinois (cat. 49).

BINDING OF ISAAC, 1963
Bronze relief
H: 83.8 cm (33″)
Collection of the artist
(cat. 48).

ALLEGORY, 1968–69, cherrywood relief, direct carving, 122 cm × 66.1 cm (48″ × 26″)
Collection of the artist (cat. 52).

PAIN, 1970, bronze, H: 49.5 cm (19½″). Collection of the artist (cat. 59).

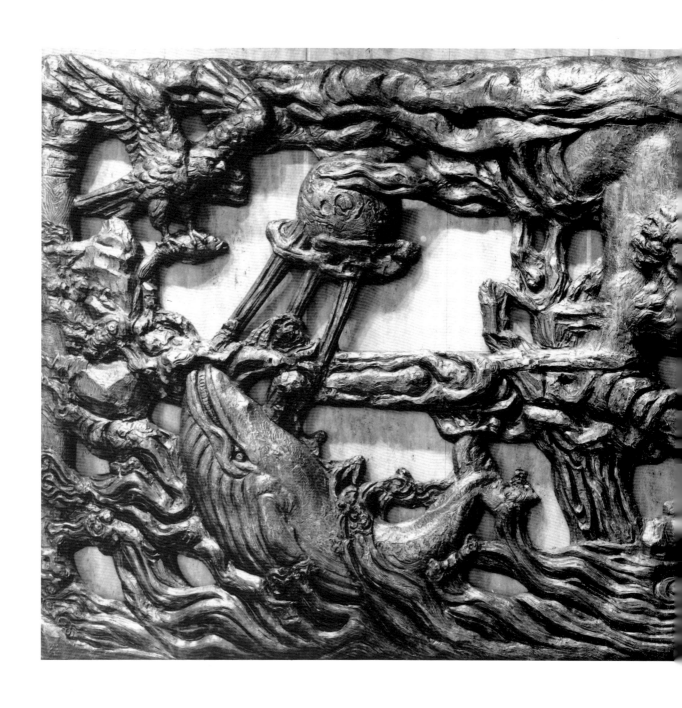

(*Above*) HYMN TO WATER, 1963–65
Bronze relief
305 cm × 732 cm (10′ × 24′)
Collection of the Chicago Central Water Filtration Plant, Chicago
(cat. 47c).

(*Right*) Milton Horn with HYMN TO WATER, 1965.

RECORDING IN THE BOOK OF LIFE, 1969, bronze relief, 66.1 cm × 69.2 cm $(26'' × 27\frac{1}{4}'')$
Collection of the artist (cat. 53).

MAN OPENS THE EARTH TO REACH THE STARS, 1970, clay, 366 cm × 305 cm (12′ × 10′)
National Bank of Congress, Charleston, West Virginia (cat. 57).

ALLEGORY: ON THE BRINK OF A PRECIPICE, 1971–73
Bronze, H: 50.2 cm $(19\frac{3}{4}'')$
Collection of the artist (cat. 61).

(*Right*) BURNING BUSH II, 1970
Bronze, H: 97.1 cm $(38\frac{1}{4}'')$
Collection of the artist (cat. 54).

(*Above and opposite page*)
GOD AND ISRAEL, 1975–79
Bronze
74.9 cm (29½″)
Collection of the artist
(cat. 67).

GLEN TETON, 1960–61
Bronze
Life size
Collection of Judge and Mrs Alfred Teton.

GAIL TETON, 1960–61
Bronze
Life size
Collection of Judge and Mrs Alfred Teton.

DR. JOSEPH H. BREWER, 1944
Bronze
Life size
Collection of Olivet College, Olivet, Michigan.

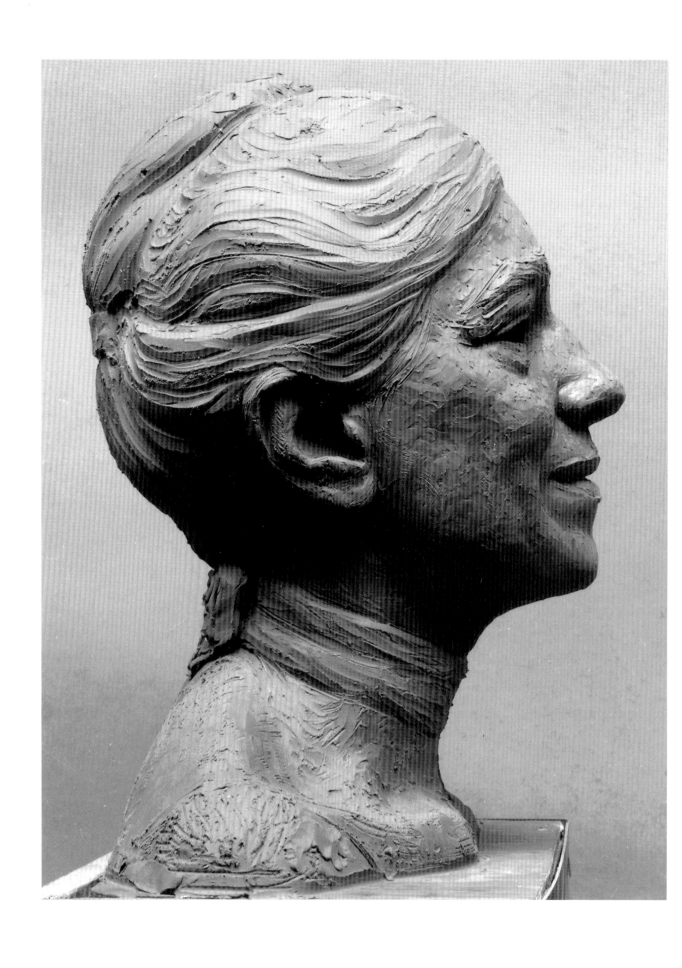

ESTELLE, 1973, bronze. H: 35.5 cm (14″)
Collection of the artist (cat. 64).

MILTON HORN, SELF PORTRAIT, 1973, bronze, H: 33 cm (13″)
Collection of the artist (cat. 63).

Figure Drawing, 1936
Ink on paper, 43.1 cm × 31.2 cm ($17'' × 12\frac{1}{4}''$)
Collection of Richard Mandeberg and Harriet Katz, Chicago
(cat. 69).

68

Figure Drawing, 1946
Ink on paper, 44.2 cm × 36.8 cm ($17\frac{3}{8}''$ × $14\frac{1}{2}''$)
Collection of the artist
(cat. 71).

Figure Drawing, 1948
Ink on paper, 36.7 cm × 26.5 cm ($14\frac{1}{2}''$ × $10\frac{1}{2}''$)
Collection of the artist
(cat. 72).

Figure Drawing, 1974
Ink on paper, 33 cm × 33 cm (13″ × 13″)
Collection of Peter and Paula Ellis, Chicago
(cat. 75).

Catalogue of the Exhibition

Unless otherwise noted, dimensions are in centimetres, followed by inches, height preceding width and depth. The drawings are sheet size. Works marked by * are illustrated in this catalogue.

Sculpture

*1 Photograph of Lentheric Perfume Salon Ceiling, 1927
Mixed media
No dimensions available
Savoy-Plaza Hotel, New York

2 FEMALE TORSO, 1927
Bronze
H: 17.3 cm ($10\frac{3}{4}''$)
Collection of the artist

3 ESTELLE, 1928
Bronze medal
DIAM: 8.2 cm ($3\frac{1}{4}''$)
Collection of the artist

4 Sketches for FOUR SEASONS, c.1920
Terra cotta
H: 15.1 cm (6'')
Collection of the artist

5 ESTHER ZIMMERER (sister of the artist), 1931
Bronze
H: 45.7 cm (18'')
Collection of the artist

*6 ESTELLE, 1933
Bronze
H: 45.7 cm (18'')
Collection of the artist

7 Photograph of HOCKEY, 1935–36
Mahogany wood relief
157 cm × 81.2 cm ($5'2'' \times 2'8''$)
HOCKEY is one of a series of 6 'Sports' panels.
Seward Park High School, New York

8 DANCER I, 1938
plaster cast
H: 35.9 cm (14'')
Collection of the artist

*9 SUMMER, 1938
Terra cotta
85.1 cm × 50.1 cm ($33\frac{1}{2}'' \times 19\frac{3}{4}''$)
Collection of the artist

10 BESSIE HORN (mother of the artist), 1938
Terra cotta
H: 45.1 cm ($17\frac{3}{4}''$)
Collection of the artist

*11 Photograph of the SPIRIT OF THE MAIL, 1938
Teakwood relief, direct carving
137 cm × 106 cm ($4'6'' \times 3'6''$)
United States Post Office, Swarthmore, Pennsylvania

12 Study for PAUL BUNYAN STRAIGHTENING OUT THE ROUND RIVER, 1941
Plaster
43.1 cm × 36.9 cm ($17'' \times 14\frac{1}{2}''$)
Collection of the artist

*13 Photograph of PAUL BUNYAN STRAIGHTENING OUT THE ROUND RIVER, 1941
Maple wood relief, direct carving
152 cm × 148 cm ($5' \times 4'9''$)
United States Post Office, Iron River, Michigan

14 JUDITH AND HOLOFERNESS, 1941
Bronze
H: 25.2 cm (10'')
Collection of Mr. and Mrs. Richard H. Freytag, Detroit, Michigan

*15 COMPOSITION, 1944
Alabaster high relief, direct carving
H: 26.6 cm ($10\frac{1}{2}''$)
Collection of the artist

*16 Photograph of Mural, C. D. Wall residence, 1943–44
Cherry wood incised relief, direct carving
204 cm × 234 cm ($6'8\frac{1}{2}'' \times 7'8\frac{1}{4}''$)
Residence was designed by architect Frank Lloyd Wright, Plymouth, Michigan.

17 MOTHER AND CHILD, 1946–47
Terra cotta
H: 22.8 cm (9'')
Collection of Peter and Paula Ellis, Chicago, Illinois

*18 JOB (Book of Job 13:15), 1947
Bronze
H: 152 cm (60'')
Collection of Tod J. and Timothy M. Kaufman, Charleston, West Virginia

19 BULL, 1947
Bronze
H: 21.5 cm ($8\frac{1}{2}''$)
Collection of the artist

*20 BATHSHEBA, 1948
Bronze
H: 35.5 cm (14'')
Collection of Dr. and Mrs. Robert Wertz, Chicago

21 TRANSCENDENCE, 1948
Bronze
H: 45.2 cm (18'')
Collection of the artist

*22 Photograph of MOTHER AND CHILD IN A GARDEN, 1948
Revised, 1967
Plaster
H: 165 cm (5' 5")
Collection of the artist

23 METAMORPHOSIS I, 1949
Black walnut wood relief mounted on wild cherry wood, direct carving
180 cm × 53.3 cm (70¾" × 21")
Collection of Peter and Paula Ellis, Chicago

*24 METAMORPHOSIS II, 1949
Walnut wood relief, direct carving
81.2 cm × 40.5 cm (32" × 16")
Collection of the artist

*25 Photograph of FAIRY TALES, 1949
Bass wood relief
W: 915 cm (30')
Blythe Park School, Riverside, Illinois

*26 HALACHA, 1950
Bronze
H: 58 cm (23")
Collection of the artist

*27 Study for 'NOT BY MIGHT, NOR BY POWER, BUT BY MY SPIRIT SAITH THE LORD OF HOSTS' (Zechariah 4:6), 1950
Plaster
179 cm × 155 cm (70½" × 61")
Collection of the artist

'NOT BY MIGHT, NOR BY POWER, BUT BY MY SPIRIT SAITH THE LORD OF HOSTS,' 1950, is a limestone relief measuring 366 cm × 305 cm (12' × 10') on the facade of West Suburban Temple Har Zion, River Forest, Illinois.

28 Study for RENAISSANCE DISSECTION, 1950–51
Plaster
45.8 cm × 45.8 cm (18" × 18")
Collection of Peter and Paula Ellis, Chicago

29 Study for MODERN OBSTETRICS, 1950–51
Plaster
45.8 cm × 45.8 cm (18' × 18')
Collection of Peter and Paula Ellis, Chicago

RENAISSANCE DISSECTION and MODERN OBSTETRICS are two of six limestone reliefs, each measuring 45.8 cm × 45.8 cm (18" × 18") from 'Medical History,' Gates Memorial Building, University of Pennsylvania Medical School, Philadelphia.

*30 CONSECRATION OF ISAIAH (Isaiah 6:6–7), 1951
Walnut wood relief, direct carving
245 cm × 120 cm (96¼" × 47¼")
Collection of the artist

*31 LAMENTATIONS I, 1951
Nickel silver
H: 41 cm (16⅛")
Collection of Barrie and Tod J. Kaufman, Charleston, West Virginia

32 EUROPA AND THE BULL, 1952–53
Bronze
H: 33 cm (13")
Collection of the artist

33 Photograph of TORAH ARK, 1953
Black walnut wood relief, direct carving
doors: 183 cm × 122 cm (6' × 4')
Temple Isaiah, Forest Hills, New York

34 THE TEACHER, THE MOTHER, THE FATHER, 1953–54
Three bronzes
each H: 73.5 cm (29")
Collection of National Congress of Parents and Teachers, Chicago

*35 TORAH ARK DOORS, 1954
Mahogany wood relief, direct carving
213 cm × 152 cm (7' × 5')
Collection of Congregation Kol Ami (formerly South Shore Temple), Chicago

36a CHICAGO RISING FROM THE LAKE, 1954
Detail 'Bovine Head'
Plaster cast
109 cm × 180 cm × 63.4 cm (43" × 71" × 25")
Collection of the artist

36b CHICAGO RISING FROM THE LAKE, 1954
Detail 'Woman's Head, "Chicago"'
Plaster cast
127 cm × 117 cm × 54.5 cm (50" × 46" × 21½")
Collection of the artist

*36c Photograph of CHICAGO RISING FROM THE LAKE, 1954
Bronze high relief
366 cm × 426 cm (12' × 14')
Façade of City of Chicago Parking Facility #1, Chicago (demolished in 1983)

*37 Photograph of HISTORY OF MEDICINE, 1954–56
Eight marble reliefs, on four pylons
223 cm × 97 cm (88" × 38")
Medical Center, University of West Virginia, Morgantown, West Virginia

*38 Photograph of ARK-REREDOS, 1957–58
Limba wood, direct carving
334 cm × 152 cm (11' × 6')
Rebecca Silling Chapel (All Faiths)
Medical Center, University of West Virginia, Morgantown, West Virginia

39 '. . . WHO WALKETH UPON THE WINGS OF THE WIND.' (Psalms 104:3), 1958
Bronze
H: 101 cm (39¾")
Collection of the artist

40 Photograph of The Jewish Federation Relief, 1958
Bronze
122 cm × 239 cm (4' × 7' 10")
Façade, Jewish Federation of Metropolitan Chicago, Chicago

41 Study for MOSES BEFORE THE BURNING BUSH, 1958
Plaster
63.5 cm × 43.1 cm (25″ × 17″)
Collection of the artist

*42 Photograph of MOSES BEFORE THE BURNING BUSH,
1959
Bronze relief
259 cm × 67 cm (8½′ × 5½′)
Temple B'nai Israel, Charleston, West Virginia

*43 Photograph of TORAH ARK DOORS, 1959–60
White oak
198 cm × 162 cm (6′6″ × 5′4″)
Temple B'nai Israel, Charleston, West Virginia

44 PINCHOS HORN (father of the artist), c.1950
Bronze
H: 37 cm (14.5″)
Collection of the artist

*45 DANCER II, 1960
Bronze
H: 47 cm (18½″)
Collection of the artist

*46 MOTHER CITY: CHICAGO EMERGING FROM THE FIRE,
1961
Plaster
H: 90.2 cm (35½″)
Collection of the artist

*47a HYMN TO WATER, 1961–65
Detail 'ADAM'
Bronze relief
H: 198 cm (78″)
Collection of the artist

47b HYMN TO WATER, 1963–65
Detail 'ABUNDANCE'
Plaster cast
122 cm × 152 cm (4′ × 5′)
Collection of the artist

47c Photograph of HYMN TO WATER, 1963–65
Bronze relief
305 cm × 732 cm (10′ × 24′)
Lobby of the Administration Building, Chicago
Central Water Filtration Plant, Chicago

*48 BINDING OF ISAAC, 1963
Bronze
H: 83.8 cm (33″)
Collection of the artist

*49 Photograph of THE ASCENSION OF RABBI JUDAH,
1963
Bronze relief
127 cm × 91.4 cm (50″ × 36″)
West Suburban Temple Har Zion
River Forest, Illinois

50 'I WILL NOT LET THEE GO' (Genesis 32:27), 1963
Bronze relief
65.4 cm × 69.8 cm (25¾″ × 27½″)
Collection of the artist

51 TRAVAIL, 1966
Walnut wood relief, direct carving
128 cm × 63.5 cm (50½″ × 25″)
Collection of the artist

*52 ALLEGORY, 1968–69
Cherry wood relief, direct carving
122 cm × 66.1 cm (48″ × 26″)
Collection of the artist

*53 RECORDING IN THE BOOK OF LIFE (Daniel 12:1),
1969
Bronze relief
66.1 cm × 69.2 cm (26″ × 27¼″)
Collection of the artist

*54 BURNING BUSH II, 1969–70
Bronze
H: 97.1 cm (38¼″)
Collection of the artist

55 BIRTH OF A POET, 1970
Bronze
H: 52.1 cm (20½″)
Collection of the artist

56 Study for MAN OPENS THE EARTH TO REACH THE
STARS, 1970
Bronze relief
31.8 cm × 26.1 cm (12½″ × 10½″)
Collection of the artist

*57 Photograph of MAN OPENS THE EARTH TO REACH
THE STARS, 1970
Clay
366 cm × 305 cm (12′ × 10′)
National Bank of Congress, Charleston, West
Virginia

58 INDEPENDENCE, 1970
Bronze
H: 107 cm (42″)
Collection of the artist

*59 PAIN, 1970
Bronze
H: 49.5 cm (19₃₂″)
Collection of the artist

60 ANDROMEDA, c.1970
Plaster cast
H: 41.9 cm (16½″)
Collection of the artist

*61 ALLEGORY: ON THE BRINK OF THE PRECIPICE,
1971–73
Bronze
H: 50.2 cm (19¾″)
Collection of the artist

62 'AM I MY BROTHER'S KEEPER?' (Genesis 4:9), 1972
Bronze
H: 38.7 cm (15¼″)
Collection of the artist

*63 MILTON HORN, SELF PORTRAIT, 1973
Bronze
H: 33 cm (13″)
Collection of the artist

*64 ESTELLE, 1973
Bronze
H: 35.5 cm (14″)
Collection of the artist

65 JUDITH AND HER MAID, 1975
Bronze
H: 82.6 cm (32½″)
Collection of the artist

66 Photograph of WOMAN WITH LUTE, 1975
Plaster
H: 157.5 cm (5½′)
Collection of the artist

*67 GOD AND ISRAEL, 1975–79
Bronze
H: 74.9 cm (29½″)
Collection of the artist

Drawings

68 Figure Drawing, 1935
Ink on paper
43.1 cm × 30.5 cm (17″ × 12″)
Collection of the artist

*69 Figure Drawing, 1936
Ink on Paper
43.1 cm × 31.2 cm (17″ × 12¼″)
Collection of Richard Mandeberg and Harriet
Katz, Chicago

70 Figure Drawing, 1938
Ink on paper
54 cm × 36.8 cm (21¼″ × 14½″)
Collection of Catherine DeJong, Chicago

*71 Figure Drawing, 1946
Ink on paper
44.2 cm × 36.8 cm (17⅜″ × 14½″)
Collection of the artist

*72 Figure Drawing, 1948
Ink on paper
36.7 cm × 26.5 cm (14½″ × 10½″)
Collection of the artist

73 Figure Drawing, 1951
Ink on paper
35.5 cm × 52.1 cm (14″ × 20½″)
Collection of Drs. Paul and Laura Mesaros,
Stubenville, Ohio

74 Figure Drawing, 1972
Ink on paper
42.9 cm × 33.6 cm (16½″ × 13¼″)
Collection of the artist

*75 Figure Drawing, 1974
Ink on paper
33 cm × 33 cm (13″ × 13″)
Collection of Peter and Paula Ellis, Chicago

Selected Exhibitions

1927
National Academy of Design, New York City. '102nd Annual Exhibition.' Group Show.

1931
New England Society of Contemporary Art, Boston. 'Exhibition of Sculpture and Drawings.' One-man exhibition.

1932
Brooklyn Museum, New York. One-man exhibition.

1932–33
The College Art Association Travelling Exhibition circulated 'Drawings by Sculptors' to the Worcester Art Museum, The Brooklyn Museum, The Dayton Art Institute, The Toledo Museum of Art, and The Rhode Island School of Design. Group show.

1934, 1937
Pennsylvania Academy of Fine Arts, Philadelphia. Annual Exhibition. Group show.

1936
Guild Art Gallery, New York City. One-man exhibition.

1940
Cleveland Museum. Annual Exhibition. Group show.

1941
Wayne University, Detroit. One-man exhibition.

1942
University of Michigan, Ann Arbor. One-man exhibition.
Layton Art Gallery, Milwaukee. 'Drawings.' One-man exhibition.

1942
Metropolitan Museum of Art, New York City. 'Artists for Victory.' Group show.

1943, 1945
Kalamazoo Institute of the Arts, Michigan. One-man exhibition.

1947
Olivet College, Michigan. One-man exhibition.

1948–49
The Jewish Museum, New York City.

1949
Philadelphia Museum of Art. 'Third Annual Exhibition of Sculpture.' Group show.

1949, 1951
Whitney Museum of American Art, New York City. Annual Exhibition. Group show.

1950
Art Institute of Chicago. '54th Annual Exhibition by Artists of Chicago and Vicinity.' Group show.

1951
Metropolitan Museum of Art, New York City. 'American Sculpture.' Group show.
The Art Institute of Chicago, 'American Federation of the Arts' travelling exhibit of the Art Institute of Chicago. Group show.

1952
The Art Institute of Chicago. 'Artists of Chicago and Vicinity.' Group show.
University of Chicago. 'Exhibition of Liturgical Art.' Group show.

1953
Contemporary Arts Museum, Houston. Group show.
University of Chicago, Renaissance Society. Annual exhibition. Group show.
University of Chicago, Rockefeller Chapel. Group show.

1953, 1954, 1955, 1977
National Institute of Arts and Letters, New York. Annual exhibition. Group show.

1954
Architectural League of New York. Group show.
Chicago Public Library. One-man exhibition.
The Art Institute of Chicago. '57th Annual Exhibition of Artists of Chicago and Vicinity.' Group show.

1955, 1956, 1957
1020 Art Center, Chicago. 'Chicago Sculptors.' Group show.

1956
Ravinia Art Festival, Highland Park, Illinois. Group show.
University of Chicago, Art Festival. Group show.

1957
American Institute of Architects, Chicago. One-man exhibition.
American Institute of Architects, Washington, D.C. One-man exhibition.

1961
University of Chicago, Renaissance Society. 'Faces and Figures.' Group show.

1964
College of Jewish Studies (now Spertus College of Judaica), Chicago. 'Jewish Ceremonial Art.' Group show.

1965
University of Chicago, Baptist Graduate Student Center. 'Sixth Annual Religious Art Show.' Group show.

Museum Collections and Public Works

National Academy of Design, New York

Brookgreen Gardens, Brookgreen, South Carolina

National Museum of American Art, Smithsonian Institution, Washington, D.C.

Temple B'nai Israel, Charleston, West Virginia

National Bank of Commerce, Charleston, West Virginia

City of Chicago

Seward Park High School, New York

Olivet College, Olivet, Michigan

Blythe Park School, Riverside, Illinois

Savoy-Plaza Hotel, New York City (demolished 1940)

University of Pennsylvania Medical School, Philadelphia

West Suburban Temple Har Zion, River Forest, Illinois

Temple Isaiah, Forest Hills, New York

National Congress of Parents & Teachers, (PTA), Chicago

West Virginia University Medical Center, Morgantown, West Virginia

Continental Can Company, Chicago (76th Street and Racine Avenue)

Women's Medical College of Pennsylvania, Philadelphia

Reynolds Memorial Hospital, Glen Dale, West Virginia

United States Post Office, Swarthmore, Pennsylvania

United States Post Office, Whitinsville, Massachusetts

United States Post Office, Iron River, Michigan

Jewish Federation of Metropolitan Chicago

Congregation Kol Ami (formerly South Shore Temple), Chicago

Milwaukee County Hospital, Wauwatosa, Wisconsin

Kenawha Bank and Trust Company, Charleston, West Virginia

West Virginia University School of Medicine, Charleston, West Virginia

Baltimore Hebrew Congregation, Maryland

Loyola University, St. Ignatius Preparatory School, Chicago

Selected Bibliography

American Sculptors, 1951. Metropolitan Museum (catalogue).

American Society of Landscape Architects Annual. 1932.

Architects Year Book. London, 1948.

Architectural Record, December, 1953, p.122; March, 1954, p.155.*

Architecture, December, 1928, p.36.*

Art, December, 1936, p.832.

Art Education Today, Teachers College, Columbia University, 1942.*

Art News, December, 1943, p.8; February, 1952, p.9; March, 1953, p.61; October, 1954, p.55; December, 1954, p.40; Summer, 1955, p.57; January, 1962, p.19.*

Arts, January 15, 1954, p.40.*

Bach, Ira J. and Mary Lackritz Gray. *Guide to Chicago Public Sculpture.* Chicago: University of Chicago Press, 1983.

Blake, Peter, ed. 'A Synagogue for Today and Tomorrow,' New York: Union of American Hebrew Congregations, 1954.

Bitterman, Eleanor. *Art in Modern Architecture.* 1952.

Brooklyn Museum Quarterly. October, 1932, p.142.*

Chicago, The Quarterly Magazine. Spring, 1965, p.44.*

'Contemporary Synagogue Design.' New York: Union of American Hebrew Congregations, 1951, plates 20a and 20b.

Creighton, Thomas H. *The Architecture of Monuments.* 1962.

Fundrauh, E. L. and Davenport, Thomas, eds. *Art in Public Places in the U.S.* Bowling Green University Press, 1975.

Goldstein, David. *Jewish Mythology.* England: Hamlin, Publ., 1987.

Hamlin, T. F., ed. *Forms and Functions in 20th Century Architecture,* Columbia University Press, 1952.

Inland Architect, A.I.A., October, 1957, p.26; December, 1961, p.12.*

Jewish Art and Civilization, Vol. 2, New York: Wigoden, Walker and Company, 1972.

Journal of American Institute of Architects, March, 1957, p.113; June, 1957, p.137; May, 1955.*

Journal CCAR, October, 1956.*

Kampf, Avram, *Contemporary Synagogue Art.* New York: Union of American Hebrew Congregations, 1966.

Narkiss, Bezalel. *Jewish Art.* Connecticut: New York Graphic Society, 1971.

Pencil Points, December, 1938.*

Philadelphia Inquirer Magazine, May, 1930; October, 1931; October, 1936; February, 1939; December 23, 1951, p.23.*

Posner, Raphael, Uri Kaptroun and Shalom Cohen. *Jewish Liturgy.* Jerusalem: Keter Press, 1975.

Redstone, Louis. *Art in Architecture.* McGraw-Hill, 1968.

Riedy, James L. *Chicago Sculpture.* Urbana: University of Illinois Press, 1981.

Roth, Cecil, ed. *Ha-Amarut Ha-Yehreidit.* Israel, 1959.

Roth, Cecil, ed. *Jewish Art.* New York: McGraw-Hill, 1961.

Roth, Cecil, ed., *Standard Jewish Encyclopedia.* New York: Doubleday, 1959.

Schultz, Bernie. 'Spirit of the Health Sciences.' *West Virginia University Alumni Magazine.* Winter and Spring 1984, pp.6–11.*

Schwartz, Earl. *Jewish Sculptors.* Tel Aviv, 1954.

Scottish Art Review. Vol. 2. Glasgow, 1948.

Sculpture, 1951. Metropolitan Museum. (Catalogue). 1951.

Sculpture by Horn. Olivet College. (Catalogue). 1948.

Sculptors Guild. (Catalogue). New York: 1952, 1953, 1954, 1960, 1961, 1962, 1963, 1964.

Sentinel's History of Chicago Jewry. Chicago: 1961, p.108.

Siegal, Arthur, ed. *Famous Chicago Buildings.* Chicago: University of Chicago Press, 1965.

Thiry, Bennett & Kamphoefner. *Churches and Temples.* Reinhold, 1953.

University of Chicago Magazine. Chicago: University of Chicago Press, March, 1961, p.8.*

West Virginia Medical Journal, February, 1957, p.85.*

* Periodicals

Lenders to the Exhibit

Congregation Kol Ami
Catherine DeJong
Paula and Peter Ellis
Mr. and Mrs. Richard H. Freytag
Milton Horn
Harriet Katz
Timothy M. Kaufman
Barrie and Tod J. Kaufman
Richard Mandeberg
Dr. Paul and Laura Mesaros
National Congress of Parents and Teachers
Dr. and Mrs. Robert Wertz

Exhibit Credits

Curators: Mark Akgulian, Olga Weiss

Spertus Museum of Judaica

Staff

Director: Morris A. Fred
Curator of Collections/Registrar: Olga Weiss
Curator of Exhibitions/Designer: Mark Akgulian
Educational Coordinator: Kathi Lieb
Assistant to the Director: Sue Shore
Assistant to the Curators: Barbara Lovell
ARTIFACT Center Coordinator: Susan Bass Marcus
Exhibit Preparators:
Jim Dorling, Tom Gengler
Support Staff:
Molly Goldberg, Zewdu Mengistu, Sari Rosen

Spertus Museum Board